D0778004

LET'S STUDY JAPANESE

LET'S STUDY JAPANESE

by JUN MAEDA

CHARLES E. TUTTLE CO., INC.
Rutland, Vermont & Tokyo, Japan

Representatives

For Continental Europe:
BOXERBOOKS, INC., Zurich

For the British Isles:
PRENTICE-HALL INTERNATIONAL, INC., London

For Australasia:
PAUL FLESCH & CO., PTY. LTD., Melbourne

For Canada:
HURTIG PUBLISHERS, Edmonton

Published by the Charles E. Tuttle Company, Inc.
of Rutland, Vermont and Tokyo, Japan
with editorial offices at Suido 1-chome, 2-6
Bunkyo-ku, Tokyo, Japan

Library of Congress Catalog Card No. 64-24949
International Standard Book No. 0-8048-0362-5
First edition, 1965
Twenty-first printing, 1976

Layout and typography by
Keiko Chiba
Printed in Japan

Table of Contents

Foreword

In this jet age, one can reach any part of the world within a day or two. It is wise for one to have some knowledge of the language of the country which he visits in order to make his trip enjoyable and worthwhile through communicating with the native people and understanding their culture.

Especially for beginners who intend to study the Japanese language, this book is written in a clear and simple yet versatile method. With approximately 350 words and examples of practical conversational usage, one may acquire a knowledge of the fundamental Japanese language from this book, so that he can express himself in simple Japanese sentences.

This book is provided with several exercises for each lesson. Also, to get acquainted with the Japanese atmosphere, the student may enjoy the illustrations which the author has provided as a visual aid. Complicated grammatical explanations are omitted in this workbook, for detailed explanations may sometimes discourage students from learning the Japanese language. Only the essential key points in pronunciation and grammar are given, and the phrases and the sentences are repeatedly presented in each lesson, so that the student can easily follow the meaning of the usage without hesitancy or discouragement.

The author hopes that the tourist as well as the student, young or old, may find this workbook helpful and enjoyable in approaching the Japanese language.

Jun Maeda

Guide to Pronunciation

There are five vowels: *a, i, u, e, o*, all of which have both short and long sounds, as noted below. The vowels, with different consonants, make up new sounds. The consonants *c, l, q, v*, and *x* do not appear, although *ch* (as in *church*) does. The vowels are pronounced as follows·

ā	approximately as in *father*
a	same sound but shorter
e	approximately as in *bed*
ē	same sound but longer
ii	approximately as *ee* in *meet*
i	same sound but shorter
ō	approximately as in *tone*
o	approximately as in *solo*
ū	approximately as *oo* in *root*
u	approximately as *oo* in *wood*

The consonants have virtually the same sounds as in English, except that *g* is always hard (as in *get*) and *r* is a sound between the English *r* and *l*. Double consonants, as in *jetto* (jet plane), *irasshaimase* (welcome, please come in), and *suitchi* (switch) must be pronounced as such, just as in English *bookkeeper* and *penknife*. Each syllable in a Japanese word should be pronounced distinctly, although in fairly rapid speech *i* and *u* are often elided, so that *desu* (am, is, are) sounds like *dess*, *deshita* (was, were) like *desh'ta*, and *arimasuka* (is there?, are there?), like *arimas'ka*. The accent in Japanese is slight and almost monotonous. However, the pitch rise and fall within phrase and sentence is recognized—e.g., *háshi* (chopsticks) and *hashí* (bridge), *káki* (oyster) and *kakí* (persimmon).

Basic Japanese Sounds

Vowels	A	I	U	E	O
Sounds	ah	ee	oo	eh	oh
With Con-sonants	ka	ki	ku	ke	ko
	sa	shi	su	se	so
	ta	chi	tsu	te	to
	na	ni	nu	ne	no
	ha	hi	fu	he	ho
	ma	mi	mu	me	mo
	ya	i	yu	e	yo
	ra	ri	ru	re	ro
	wa	i	u	e	o
					n
	ga	gi	gu	ge	go
	za	ji	zu	ze	zo
	da	ji	zu	de	do
	ba	bi	bu	be	bo
	pa	pi	pu	pe	po
	kya	—	kyu	—	kyo
	sha	—	shu	—	sho
	cha	—	chu	—	cho

pya	—	pyu	—	pyo
nya	—	nyu	—	nyo
mya	—	myu	—	myo
rya	—	ryu	—	ryo
hya	—	hyu	—	hyo
gya	—	gyu	—	gyo
bya	—	byu	—	byo
ja	—	ju	—	jo

LESSON 1

What Is This?

Kore-wa nan desuka.	What is this? (What are these?)
Kore-wa hon desu.	This is a book.
Kore-wa empitsu desu.	This is a pencil.
Kore-wa inu desu.	This is a dog.
Kore-wa hana desu.	This is a flower. (These are flowers.)

hon

empitsu

inu

hana

kore	this (sometimes *these*)
-wa	(postposition for nominative case, emphasizing subject)
nan, nani	what?
desu	is, are, am
-ka	(Adding *ka* at the end of a sentence makes the sentence interrogative.)
hon	book
empitsu	pencil
inu	dog
hana	flower (flowers)
Hai, sō desu.	Yes, it is (they are).
Iie, sō de-arimasen.	No, it is (they are) not.
Kore-wa jidōsha desu-ka.	Is this a car?

jidōsha

Hai, sō desu.	Yes, it is.
Kore-wa hikōki desu-ka.	Is this an airplane?

hikōki

Hai, sō desu.	Yes, it is.
Kore-wa inu desuka.	Is this a dog?

 neko

Iie, sō de-arimasen.	No, it is not. This is a
Kore-wa neko desu.	cat.
Kore-wa hana desuka.	Is this (are these) a
	flower (flowers)?

 kudamono

Iie, sō de-arimasen.	No, it is (they are) not.
Kore-wa kudamono	This is fruit.
desu.	
Kore-wa kutsu desu-	Are these shoes?
ka.	

geta

Iie, sō de-arimasen.	No, they are not. These
Kore-wa geta desu.	are wooden clogs.

hai	yes
iie	no
de-arimasen	is not, are not
jidōsha	car (automobile)
hikōki	airplane

15

neko   cat
kudamono   fruit
kutsu   shoes
geta   wooden clogs

NOTE: In Japanese the same form serves for the sin-
gular and plural of nouns and verbs. The context usually makes clear which is meant. Occasionally, when it is
necessary to be quite explicit, a pluralizing suffix can be
added to nouns (and is frequently added to pronouns),
but it is not essential for the beginner to be concerned
about this usage.

EXERCISE

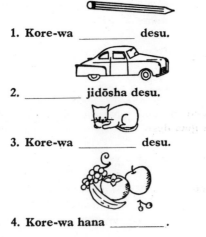

1. Kore-wa _____ desu.

2. _____ jidōsha desu.

3. Kore-wa _____ desu.

4. Kore-wa hana _____ .

5. _____ kudamono de-arimasen.

6. Kore-wa jidōsha _____.

7. _____ desu.

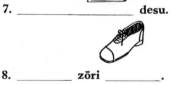

8. _____ zōri _____.

LESSON 2

Where Are You Going?

Anata-wa doko-e iki-masuka (yukimasu-ka).

Where are you going?

Tōkyō-eki

Watakushi-wa Tōkyō Eki-e ikimasu.

I am going to Tokyo Station.

yūbinkyoku

Watakushi-wa yūbin-kyoku-e ikimasu.

I am going to the post office.

18

uchi

Watakushi-wa uchi-e ikimasu. I am going home.

gakkō

Watakushi-wa gakkō-e ikimasu. I am going to school.

anata-wa	you (nominative)
doko, doko-e	where?
-e	to (postposition indicating direction)
ikimasu (sometimes **yukimasu**)	go, goes
watakushi-wa (less formally and commonly, **watashi-wa**)	I (with nominative postposition)
Tōkyō Eki	Tokyo Station
yūbinkyoku	post office
uchi	home, house
gakkō	school

19

Doko desuka.	Where is it?
Koko desu. (Koko-ni arimasu.)	It is here. (Here it is. Right here.)
Soko desu. (Soko-ni arimasu.)	There it is. (It is over there. Over there.)
Nimotsu-wa doko de-suka.	Where is the luggage (package)?

nimotsu

Koko desu.	It is here.
Shimbun-wa doko de-suka.	Where is the news-paper?

shimbun

Soko desu.	It is over there.
Heya-wa doko desu-ka.	Where is the room?

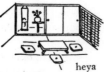

heya

Koko desu.	It is here.
Pen-wa doko desuka.	Where is the pen?

pen

Soko desu.	It is over there.
koko	here
soko	there, over there
nimotsu	luggage, package
shimbun	newspaper
heya	room
pen	pen

EXERCISE

1. Anata-wa doko-e ikimasuka.

2. _____.

3. _____.

4. _____   _____   _____ .

5. Pen-wa doko desuka.   _____

_____ .

6. Nimotsu-wa doko desuka.   _____

_____ .

LESSON 3

Can You Do It?

Anata-wa dekimasu-ka.	Can you do (speak, read, write, etc.)?
Hai, dekimasu.	Yes, I can.
Iie, dekimasen.	No, I can't.
Anata-wa Eigo-ga de-kimasuka.	Can you speak English?

Eigo

Hai, dekimasu.	Yes, I can.
Anata-wa Nihongo-ga dekimasuka.	Can you speak Japanese?

Nihongo

Iie, dekimasen.	No, I can't.
Anata-wa ryōri-ga de-kimasuka.	Can you cook?

23

ryōri

Hai, dekimasu.   Yes, I can.
Anata-wa yomu-koto-   Can you read?
ga dekimasuka.

yomu-koto

Anata-wa Nihongo-o   Can you write Japanese?
kaku-koto-ga deki-
masu.

kaku-koto

Iie, dekimasen.   No, I can't.
Anata-wa Nihon ryō-   Can you eat Japanese
ri-o taberu-koto-ga-   food (cooking)?
dekimasuka.

taberu-koto

Hai, dekimasu.   Yes, I can.

dekimasu   can do (speak, read,
                           write, etc.)

24

dekimasen	cannot do (speak, read, write, etc.)
Eigo	English language
-ga	(nominative postposition less emphatic than *wa*)
Nihongo	Japanese language
ryōri	cooking (noun)
yomu-koto	to read, reading (noun)
kaku-koto	to write, writing (noun)
taberu-koto	to eat, eating (noun)
Nihon ryōri	Japanese food (dishes, cooking)
-o	(postposition for objective case)

EXERCISE

1. Anata-wa Eigo-ga dekimasuka.

   _____   _____ .

2. Anata-wa Nihongo-ga dekimasuka.

   _____   _____ .

3. Anata-wa gorufu-ga dekimasuka.

   _____   _____ .

4. Anata-wa piano-ga dekimasuka.

   _____   _____ .

5. Anata-wa Nihongo-o yomu-koto-ga dekimasuka.   _____   _____ .

6. Anata-wa Eigo-o kaku-koto-ga dekimasuka.   _____   _____ .

7. Anata-wa Nihon ryōri-o taberu-koto-ga dekimasuka. _____ _____.

8. Anata-wa Nihon-e iku-koto-ga dekimasuka. _____ _____.

9. Anata-wa uchi-e kuru-koto-ga dekimasuka. _____ _____.

10. Anata-wa yūbinkyoku-e iku-koto-ga dekimasuka. _____ _____.

gorufu	golf
piano	piano
Nihon	Japan
iku-koto	to go, going (noun)
kuru-koto	to come, coming (noun)

LESSON 4

Do You Have It?

Anata-wa . . . motte-imasuka.	Do you have . . . ?
Hai, motte-imasu.	Yes, (I) have.
Iie, motte-imasen.	No, I haven't. No, I don't (have).
Anata-wa kippu-o motte-imasuka.	Do you have a ticket?

kippu

Hai, motte-imasu.	Yes, I have.
Anata-wa tokei-o motte-imasuka.	Do you have a watch (clock)?

tokei

Hai, motte-imasu.	Yes, I have.
Anata-wa bōshi-o motte-imasuka.	Do you have a hat?

27

bōshi

Iie, motte-imasen.	No, I haven't.
Anata-wa kitte-o mot-te-imasuka.	Do you have a stamp (some stamps)?

 kitte

Anata-wa kasa-o mot-te-imasuka.	Do you have an umbrella?

 kasa

motte-imasu	have, has
motte-imasen	haven't, hasn't
kippu	ticket
tokei	watch, clock
bōshi	hat
kitte	stamp
kasa	umbrella

EXERCISE

1. **Anata-wa kasa-o motte-imasuka.**

_____ _____.

2. Anata-wa tokei-o motte-imasuka.

_____ _____.

3. Anata-wa kitte-o motte-imasuka.

_____ _____.

4. Anata-wa pen-o motte-imasuka.

_____ _____.

5. Anata-wa bōshi-o motte-imasuka.

_____ _____.

29

LESSON 5

Do You Like It?

Anata-wa . . . -ga suki desuka.	Do you like . . . ?
Hai, suki desu.	Yes, I do. (Yes, I like it.)
Iie, suki de-arimasen. Kirai desu.	No, I don't. (No, I don't like it.) I dislike it.
Anata-wa Nihon-ga suki desuka.	Do you like Japan?

Nihon

Hai, suki desu.	Yes, I do.
Anata-wa ongaku-ga suki desuka.	Do you like music?

ongaku

Hai, suki desu.	Yes, I do.
Anata-wa nezumi-ga suki desuka.	Do you like mice (rats)?

nezumi

Iie, suki de-arimasen.	No, I don't.
Anata-wa mushi-ga suki desuka.	Do you like insects?

mushi

Iie, kirai desu.	No, I dislike them.

suki desu	like, likes
suki de-arimasen	do not like, does not like
kirai desu	dislike, dislikes
ongaku	music
nezumi	mouse, rat
mushi	insect

EXERCISE

1. **Anata-wa ringo-ga suki desuka.**

ringo

31

———————— ————.

2. Anata-wa sakana-ga suki desuka.

sakana

———————— ————.

3. Anata-wa tori-ga suki desuka.

tori

———————— ————.

4. Anata-wa kōhii-ga suki desuka.

kōhii

———————— ————.

5. Anata-wa kisha-ga suki desuka.

kisha

———————— ————.

6. Anata-wa Nihon ningyō-ga suki desuka.

Nihon-ningyō

ringo	apple
sakana	fish
tori	bird
kōhii	coffee
kisha	train
Nihon ningyō	Japanese doll

LESSON 6

Please and Thank You

Dōzo watakushi-ni . . . kudasai.   Please give me . . .

Dōzo watakushi-ni o-mizu-o kudasai.   Please give me some (a drink of) water.

Dōzo watakushi-ni o-saji-o kudasai.   Please give me a spoon.

Dōzo watakushi-ni isu-o kudasai.   Please give me a chair.

Dōzo watakushi-ni kami-o kudasai.   Please give me some paper.

Dōzo watakushi-ni uwagi-o kudasai.   Please give me a jacket (coat).

Arigatō-gozaimasu.   Thank you.

dōzo	please
watakushi-ni	to me
-ni	to, for, in (objective postposition)
o-mizu, mizu (o- is an honorific prefix used for politeness)	water
o-saji, saji	spoon
isu	chair
kami	paper
uwagi	jacket, coat
... kudasai	(please) give me

EXERCISE

1. Dōzo watakushi-ni _____ kudasai.
Arigatō-gozaimasu.

2. Dōzo _____ hon-o _____. Arigatō-gozaimasu.

3. _____ watakushi-ni kitte-o _____.
Dōmo arigatō-gozaimasu.

4. Dōzo _____ _____ kudasai. Dōmo arigatō-gozaimasu.

5. _____ _____ tabako-o _____.
   Dōmo arigatō-gozaimasu.

6. Dōzo watakushi-ni _____ kudasai.
   _____ arigatō-gozaimasu.

Arigatō-gozaimasu.	Thank you.
Arigatō (less formal).	Thank you.
dōmo	very, very much
tabako	cigarette
haizara	ashtray

37

LESSON 7

Numbers

Kazu	Numbers
ichi, hitotsu	1
ni, futatsu	2
san, mittsu	3
shi, yottsu	4
go, itsutsu	5
roku, muttsu	6
shichi, nana, nanatsu	7
hachi, yattsu	8
ku, kyū, kokonotsu	9
jū, tō	10
jū-ichi	11
jū-ni	12
jū-san	13
jū-shi, jū-yon	14
jū-go	15
jū-roku	16
jū-shichi	17
jū-hachi	18
jū-ku	19
ni-jū	20

ni-jū-ichi	21
san-jū	30
shi-jū, yon-jū	40
go-jū	50
roku-jū	60
nana-jū, shichi-jū	70
hachi-jū	80
ku-jū	90
hyaku	100
hyaku-ichi	101
hyaku-go-jū	150
ni-hyaku	200
sambyaku (*n-h* becomes *mb*)	300
yon-hyaku	400
go-hyaku	500
roppyaku (*ku-h* becomes *pp*)	600
nana-hyaku, shichi-hyaku	700
happyaku (*chi-h* becomes *pp*)	800
kyū-hyaku	900
sen	1,000
go-sen	5,000
ichi-man	10,000
samman (*n-m* becomes *mm*)	30,000
jū-man	100,000
hyaku-man	1,000,000

NOTE: In the numbers from 1 through 10, the last one given in each case is the number used in counting things

—e.g., *bōshi hitotsu* or *hitotsu-no bōshi* (one hat), *isu futatsu* or *futatsu-no isu* (two chairs), etc. In counting people, the numbers are used as follows:

hitori	one person
futari	two persons, two people
san-nin	three people
yo-nin	four people
go-nin	five people
roku-nin	six people
shichi-nin	seven people
hachi-nin	eight people
ku-nin	nine people
tō-nin, jū-nin	ten people

From 10 on, the suffix *-nin* is added to the number as given in the first table above, except that *yo* is always used instead of *shi* for 4 in counting people; hence *ni-jū-yo-nin*: 24 people.

EXERCISE

Anata-wa kazu-o yomu-koto-ga dekimasuka. Can you read (the) numbers?

1	2	3	4	5	6
7	8	9	10	20	55
70	93	100	120	350	510
600	650	700	830	900	980
1,000	1,500	1,950	1,964	5,000	10,000

LESSON 8

What Time Is It?

Nan-ji desuka.	What time is it?
nan-ji	what time?
-ji	hours, o'clock
ichi-ji	one o'clock
yo-ji (*yo*, not *shi*, in telling time)	four o'clock
han	half, half past
fun (pun)	minute
ippun (*chi-f* becomes *pp*)	one minute
ni-fun	two minutes
sampun (*n-f* becomes *mp*)	three minutes
yompun (*n-f* becomes *mp*)	four minutes
go-fun	five minutes
roppun (*ku-f* becomes *pp*)	six minutes
shichi-fun, nana-fun	seven minutes
hachi-fun	eight minutes
kyū-fun	nine minutes

jippun (*ū-f* becomes *ipp*)   ten minutes
jū-go-fun   fifteen minutes
ni-jippun   twenty minutes
san-jippun   thirty minutes
sugi   after, past (in telling time)
mae   before, to (in telling time)

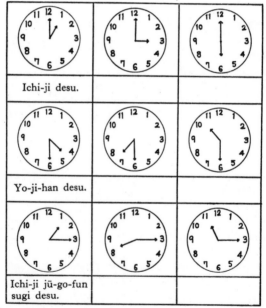

Ichi-ji desu.		
Yo-ji-han desu.		
Ichi-ji jū-go-fun sugi desu.		

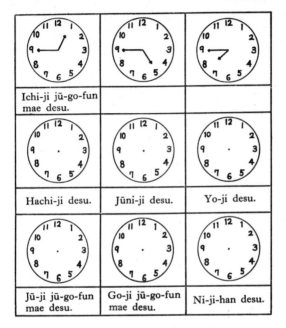

Ichi-ji jū-go-fun mae desu.		
Hachi-ji desu.	Jūni-ji desu.	Yo-ji desu.
Jū-ji jū-go-fun mae desu.	Go-ji jū-go-fun mae desu.	Ni-ji-han desu.

LESSON 9

What Day Is Today?

Kyō-wa nan nichi de-suka.	What day of the month is it today?
Kyō-wa . . . desu.	Today is the . . .
Kinō-wa nan nichi de-shitaka.	What day of the month was it yesterday?
Asu-wa (ashita-wa) nan nichi desuka.	What day of the month is it tomorrow?
Kyō-wa nan nichi de-suka.	What day of the month is it today?
Kyō-wa jū-roku nichi desu.	Today is the sixteenth.
Kino-wa nan nichi deshitaka.	What day of the month was it yesterday?
Kinō-wa jū-go nichi deshita.	Yesterday was the fifteenth.
Asu-wa nan nichi de-suka.	What day of the month is it tomorrow?
Asu-wa jū-shichi ni-chi desu.	Tomorrow is the seventeenth.

kyō	today
nan	what?
nichi	day (of the month)
kinō	yesterday
deshita	was, were
asu, ashita	tomorrow

Days of the month:

tsuitachi	first
futsuka	second
mikka	third
yokka	fourth
itsuka	fifth
muika	sixth
nanoka	seventh
yōka	eighth
kokonoka	ninth
tōka	tenth
jū-ichi nichi	eleventh
jū-ni nichi	twelfth
jū-san nichi	thirteenth
jū-yokka	fourteenth
jū-go nichi	fifteenth
jū-roku nichi	sixteenth
jū-shichi nichi	seventeenth
jū-hachi nichi	eighteenth
jū-ku nichi	nineteenth
hatsuka	twentieth

ni-jū-ichi nichi	twenty-first
ni-jū-ni nichi	twenty-second
ni-jū-san nichi	twenty-third
ni-jū-yokka	twenty-fourth
ni-jū-go nichi	twenty-fifth
ni-jū-roku nichi	twenty-sixth
ni-jū-shichi nichi	twenty-seventh
ni-jū-hachi nichi	twenty-eighth
ni-jū-ku nichi	twenty-ninth
san-jū nichi	thirtieth
san-jū-ichi nichi	thirty-first

Kyō-wa nani yōbi de-suka.	What day of the week is it today?
Kyō-wa Getsu-yōbi desu.	Today is Monday.
Kinō-wa nani yōbi deshitaka.	What day of the week was it yesterday?
Kinō-wa Nichi-yōbi deshita.	Yesterday was Sunday.
Asu-wa nani yōbi de-suka.	What day of the week is it tomorrow?
Asu-wa Ka-yōbi desu.	Tomorrow is Tuesday.

yōbi	day of the week
shū	week
konshū	this week
senshū	last week

raishū next week
kyūjitsu holiday

Tsuki

S	M	T	W	T	F	S
1	2	3	4	5	6	7
8	9	10	11	12	13	14
15	16	17	18	19	20	

Shū

日	月	火	水	木	金	土
				5	6	7
8	9	10	11	12		

日	Nichi-yōbi	Sunday
月	Getsu-yōbi	Monday
火	Ka-yōbi	Tuesday
水	Sui-yōbi	Wednesday
木	Moku-yōbi	Thursday
金	Kin-yōbi	Friday
土	Do-yōbi	Saturday
休日	Kyūjitsu	Holiday

EXERCISE

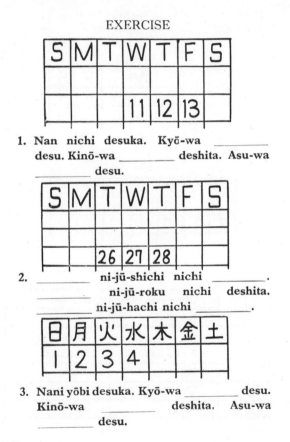

S	M	T	W	T	F	S
				11	12	13

1. Nan nichi desuka. Kyō-wa _____
   desu. Kinō-wa _____ deshita. Asu-wa
   _____ desu.

S	M	T	W	T	F	S
		26	27	28		

2. _____ ni-jū-shichi nichi _____.
   _____ ni-jū-roku nichi deshita.
   _____ ni-jū-hachi nichi _____.

日	月	火	水	木	金	土
1	2	3	4			

3. Nani yōbi desuka. Kyō-wa _____ desu.
   Kinō-wa _____ deshita. Asu-wa
   _____ desu.

日	月	火	水	木	金	土
		1	2	3	4	5

4. Kyō-wa   nan   niohi   desuka.   Kyō-wa
   _____ desu. Kyō-wa nani yōbi desuka.
   Kyō-wa _____ desu. Nichi-yōbi-wa
   _____ desu.

LESSON 10

Seasons and Months

Kisetsu to Tsuki		Seasons and Months	
haru:	**San-gatsu**	spring:	March
	Shi-gatsu		April
	Go-gatsu		May
natsu:	**Roku-gatsu**	summer:	June
	Shichi-gatsu		July
	Hachi-gatsu		August
aki:	**Ku-gatsu**	autumn:	September
	Jū-gatsu		October
	Jū-ichi-gatsu		November
fuyu:	**Jū-ni-gatsu**	winter:	December
	Ichi-gatsu		January
	Ni-gatsu		February

kongetsu	this month
sengetsu	last month
raigetsu	next month

NOTE: The word "month" is expressed in three ways in Japanese: *tsuki*, *getsu*, and *gatsu*, the last two being used as suffixes. In giving the number of months (one month, two months, etc.), the easiest system for the beginner is as follows:

ikkagetsu	one month
nikagetsu	two months
sankagetsu	three months
yonkagetsu	four months
gokagetsu	five months
rokkagetsu	six months
nanakagetsu	seven months
hachikagetsu	eight months
kyūkagetsu	nine months
jikkagetsu	ten months
jū-ikkagetsu	eleven months
jū-nikagetsu	twelve months

Kikō-wa ikaga de-suka.	How is the climate? (What is the climate like?)
Haru-wa atatakai de-su.	Spring is warm. (It is warm in spring.)

LET'S STUDY JAPANESE

Natsu-wa atsui desu. Summer is hot. (It is hot in summer.)

Aki-wa suzushii desu. Autumn is cool. (It is cool in autumn.)

Fuyu-wa samui desu. Winter is cold. (It is cold in winter.)

kikō	climate
ikaga	how?
haru	spring
atatakai	warm
natsu	summer
atsui	hot
aki	autumn
suzushii	cool
fuyu	winter
samui	cold

EXERCISE

Tadashii kotae-wa do-chira desuka. Which is the correct answer?

Fuyu-wa { samui / atsui / suzushii } **desu.**

Natsu-wa { atatakai / samui / atsui } **desu.**

52

Aki-wa	{ samui / suzushii / atatakai }	desu.
Fuyu-wa	{ atsui / samui / atatakai }	desu.

Go-gatsu	$\longrightarrow$	May
Ichi-gatsu		August
Roku-gatsu		December
Hachi-gatsu		June
Jū-ni-gatsu		January

LESSON 11

Greetings and Everyday Expressions

Aisatsu   Greetings

Asa
Ohayō-gozaimasu.

(asa, gozen) Ohayō-   (morning, A.M.) Good
gozaimasu.   morning.

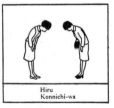

Hiru
Konnichi-wa

(hiru, gogo) Konnichi-   (afternoon, P.M.) Good
wa.   day. (Hello. Good
                       afternoon.)

(**yūgata, ban**) **Kom-ban-wa.** (evening) Good evening.

(**yoru**) **Oyasumi-na-sai.** (night) Good night.

Sayonara. Goodbye.

Irasshaimase.   Welcome. Please come
                                 in.

Nichijō Hyōgen   Everyday Expressions
Itadakimasu.   (This expression is used
                                 before eating. It is
                                 somewhat similar to
   "Thank you" in re-
                                 sponse to "Please help
                                 yourself.")

Gochisō-sama.   (This expression is used
                                 after eating. It is
                                 something like "It was
   delicious" or "It was
                                 a treat.")

Gomen-nasai.

I am sorry. (Excuse me. Pardon me.)

Gomen-nasai

Omedetō-gozaimasu.

Congratulations! (This expression is used on any happy occasion such as a wedding, a birthday, graduation, baby's arrival, New Year's Day, etc.)

Omedetō-gozaimasu

nichijō

everyday (adjective)

hyōgen

expressions

LESSON 12

What Are You?

Anata-no namae-wa nan desuka.	What is your name?
Anata-wa . . . desuka.	Are you a (an) . . . ?
Hai, sō desu.	Yes, I am.
Iie, watakushi-wa . . . desu.	No, I am a (an) . . .
Anata-wa Amerika-jin desuka.	Are you an American?

Amerika-jin

Hai, sō desu.	Yes, I am.
Anata-wa Nihon-jin desuka.	Are you a Japanese?

Nihon-jin

| Hai, sō desu. | Yes, I am. |
| Anata-wa sensei de-suka. | Are you a teacher? |

gakusei

| Iie, watakushi-wa gakusei desu. | No, I am student. |
| Anata-wa gakusei de-suka. | Are you a student? |

sensei

| Iie, watakushi-wa sensei desu. | No, I am a teacher. |
| Anata-no jūsho-o kudasai. | Please give me your address. |

anata-no	your
namae	name
Amerika-jin	an American, American people
Nihon-jin	a Japanese, Japanese people

59

sensei   teacher
gakusei   student
jūsho   address

EXERCISE

1. **Anata-wa isha desuka.** _____

isha

_____ _____.

2. **Anata-wa o-mawari-san desuka.**

junsa
o-mawari-san

_____ _____ _____.

3. **Anata-wa isha desuka.** _____

bijinesu-man

_____ _____.

4. **Anata-wa okusan desuka.** _____

60

okusan

_____ _____.

isha	doctor
o-mawari-san	policeman
bijinesu-man	businessman
okusan	wife, Mrs.

LESSON 13

Food

Tabemono	Food
Dōzo meshi-agatte kudasai.	Please help yourself. (Please do eat.)

Arigatō-gozaimasu. Itadakimasu.	Thank you, I shall.

 gohan

Gohan-wa shiroi desu.	Cooked rice is white.

 niku

Niku-wa akai desu.	(The) meat is red.

pan

Pan-wa oishii desu.	(The) bread is delicious.

tamago

Tamago-wa marui desu. — Eggs are round. (An egg is round.)

o-tōfu

O-tōfu-wa shikakui desu. — Bean curd is square. (Bean curd comes in square cakes.)

yasai

Yasai-wa shinsen de-su. — The vegetables are fresh.

tabemono	food
Meshi-agatte kuda-sai.	Please help yourself. (Please do eat.)
gohan	cooked rice
shiroi	white
niku	meat
akai	red
pan	bread
oishii	tasty, delicious
tamago	egg

marui	round
o-tōfu, tōfu	bean curd
shikakui	square
yasai	vegetable, vegetables
shinsen	fresh
o-satō, satō	sugar

o-satō
O-satō-wa amai desu.

amai	sweet
o-shio, shio	salt

o-shio
O-shio-wa karai desu.

karai	salty, peppery, spicy
gyūnyū, miruku	milk

gyūnyū, miruku
Gyūnyū-wa tsumetai desu.

tsumetai	cold, cool

o-cha
O-cha-wa atsui desu.

o-cha, cha (usually   tea
  o-cha)

atsui   hot

tōsuto   toast

tōsuto
bata
Bata-wa yawarakai desu.

bata   butter

yawarakai   soft

o-sembei, sembei   Japanese rice crackers

o-sembei
O-sembei-wa katai desu.

katai   hard, crisp

EXERCISE

65

1. **O-satō-wa** _____ **desu.**

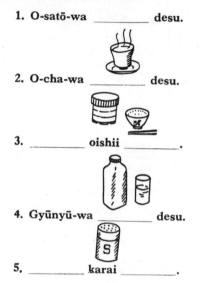

2. **O-cha-wa** _____ **desu.**

3. _____ **oishii** _____.

4. **Gyūnyū-wa** _____ **desu.**

5. _____ **karai** _____.

LESSON 14

How Is the Weather?

O-tenki-wa dō desuka.   How is the weather?

Ii (yoi) o-tenki desu.   The weather is good.

Warui o-tenki desu.   The weather is bad.
Ame desu.   It is raining.

Kumori desu.   It is cloudy.

67

Yuki desu.	It is snowing.

o-tenki, tenki	weather
dō	how?
ii (sometimes **yoi**)	good
warui	bad
ame	rain
kumori	cloudy
yuki	snow

EXERCISE

O-tenki-wa dō desuka. Tadashii kotae-wa dochira desuka.

1. **Yuki desu.**
   Ii o-tenki desu.
   Ame desu.

2. **Kumori desu.**
   Warui o-tenki desu.
   Ii o-tenki desu.

3. Ame desu.
   Kumori desu.
   Yuki desu.

4. Ii o-tenki desu.
   Warui o-tenki desu.
   Yuki desu.

LESSON 15

Review

Fukushū	Review
1. Kyō-wa nan nichi desuka.	1. _____ _____ _____.
2. Kyō-wa nani yōbi desuka.	2. _____ _____ _____.
3. Kyō-no o-tenki-wa dō desuka.	3. _____ _____ _____.

4. Tadashii kotae-wa dochira desuka.

Komban-wa.	Good evening.
Oyasumi-nasai.	Goodbye.
Konnichi-wa.	Congratulations.
Sayonara.	Thank you.
Irasshaimase.	Welcome. (Please come in.)
Omedetō-gozaima-su.	Good day. (Hello. Good afternoon.)
Arigatō-gozaimasu.	Good morning.
Gomen-nasai.	Good night.
Ohayō-gozaimasu.	I am sorry. (Excuse me. Pardon me.)

5. Tadashii kazu-wa dochira desuka.

roku	9	7	4	6	2
ni-jū-san	33	21	15	11	23
go-hyaku	211	510	100	500	300
hachi-jū-hachi	24	36	88	49	18
sen-kyū-hyaku- roku-jū-san	185	1226	1963	1684	1953

LET'S STUDY JAPANESE

LESSON 16

Let's Go Shopping

Kaimono-ni ikimashō.	Let's go shopping.
Kore-wa ikura desuka.	How much is this?
Are-wa ikura desuka.	How much is that (over there)?
Sore-wa ikura desuka.	How much is that?
Sore-wa hyaku en desu.	That (it) is 100 yen.

kaimono	shopping
-ni	for, to, at, in
ikimashō	let's go
kore	this (pronoun)
are	that (pronoun, for distant objects)
sore	that (pronoun, for non-distant objects)
ikura	how much?
en	yen (360 yen=$1.00)

1. **Kore-wa ikura desuka.**

mikan

Kore-wa jū-en desu.

2. **Are-wa ikura desuka.**

shinju

Are-wa ichi-man en desu.

3. **Sore-wa ikura desuka.**

shashinki
kamera

Sore-wa nana-sen-ni-hyaku en desu.

4. **Kore-wa ikura desuka.**

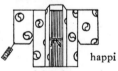

happi

Kore-wa sen-ni-hyaku en desu.

EXERCISE

Anata-wa kaimono-ni ikimasu.

1. **Kore-wa _____ desuka.**

ningyō

Sore-wa _____ _____ desu.

2. Hagaki-wa _____ desuka.

hagaki

Sore-wa _____ _____ desu.

3. _____ ikura _____.

kabin

_____ **go-hyaku en** _____.

4. _____ ikura _____.

shokki

_____ **sen en** _____.

ningyō	doll
hagaki	postcard
kabin	vase
shokki	dinnerware

74

LESSON 17

How Are You?

Gokigen ikaga desu-ka.   How are you?

Watakushi-wa genki desu.   I am well. (I am fine.)

Watakushi-wa byōki desu. Atama-ga itai desu.   I am ill. I have a head-ache. (My head aches.)

Ha-ga itai desu.

I have a toothache. (My tooth aches.)

Watakushi-wa byōki desu. O-naka-ga itai desu.

I am ill. I have a stomach ache. (My stomach aches.)

gokigen	feeling, state of health
genki	well, fine, healthy
byōki	ill, illness
atama	head
-ga	(nominative postposition, less emphatic than *wa*)
itai	painful, aching
ha	tooth, teeth
o-naka	stomach

LESSON 18

Parts of the Body

Karada-no Bubun	Parts of the Body
karada	body
-no	of (postposition for possessive case)
bubun	parts

me   me   eye

hana   hana   nose

mimi   mimi   ear

ude   ude   arm

te   te   hand

yubi   yubi   finger

77

LET'S STUDY JAPANESE

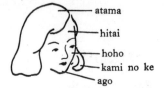

atama	head
hitai	forehead
hoho	cheek
kami-no-ke, ke	hair
ago	chin

kuchi		mouth
ha	ha	teeth
shita	shita	tongue
ashi	ashi	foot, leg
hiza	hiza	knee
ashi-no-yubi	ashi-no yubi	toes

78

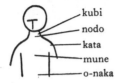

kubi	neck
nodo	throat
kata	shoulder
mune	chest
o-naka	stomach

EXERCISE

Kore-wa nan desuka. Tadashii kotae-o e-no soba-ni kaite kudasai. What is this? Please write the correct answer next to the picture.

1. **Kore-wa me desu.**

2. **Kore-wa kuchi desu.**

3. **Kore-wa hana desu.**

4. **Kore-wa mimi desu.**

5. **Kore-wa te desu.**

6. **Kore-wa ha desu.**

7. **Kore-wa kami-no-ke desu.**

8. **Kore-wa ashi desu.**

9. **Kore-wa hoho desu.**

tadashii	correct, right
kotae	answer
-o	(postposition, objective case)
e	picture
-no	(postposition, possessive case)
soba-ni	next to
kaite kudasai	please write

LESSON 19

You and I, Your and My

Watakushi-wa . . .	I . . .
Anata-wa . . .	You . . .
watakushi-no . . .	my
anata-no . . .	your

tomodachi

Watakushi-wa anata-no tomodachi desu. — I am your friend.

Anata-wa watakushi-no tomodachi desu. — You are my friend.

gaido

Watakushi-wa anata-no gaido desu. — I am your guide.

Anata-wa watakushi-no gaido desu.	You are my guide.
Kore-wa anata-no aka-chan desuka.	Is this your baby?

aka-chan

Kore-wa watakushi-no aka-chan desu.	This is my baby.

tomodachi (sometimes **o-tomodachi**)	friend
gaido	guide
aka-chan	baby

EXERCISE

1. **Kore-wa watakushi-no** _____

_____.

2. Anata-wa _____ _____ desu.

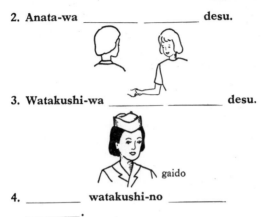

gaido

3. Watakushi-wa _____ _____ desu.

4. _____ watakushi-no _____
_____ .

LESSON 20

This and That

kore-wa	this (nominative)
kono	this (adjective)
are-wa	that (nominative, for distant objects)
ano	that (adjective, for distant objects)
sore-wa	that (nominative, for non-distant objects)
sono	that (adjective, for non-distant objects)

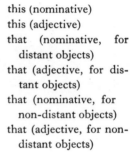

kawaii yōfuku

1. **Kore-wa yōfuku desu. Kono yōfuku-wa kawaii desu.**

utsukushii e

2. **Are-wa e desu. Ano e-wa utsukushii desu.**

hoteru
yūmei

3. **Sore-wa hoteru desu. Sono hoteru-wa yūmei desu.**

to
deguchi

4. **Kore-wa to desu. Kono to-wa deguchi desu. Iriguchi wa doko desuka.**

yōfuku	dress, clothes (Western style)
kawaii	cute, pretty
e	picture
utsukushii	beautiful
hoteru	hotel
yūmei	famous
to	door
deguchi	exit
iriguchi	entrance

EXERCISE

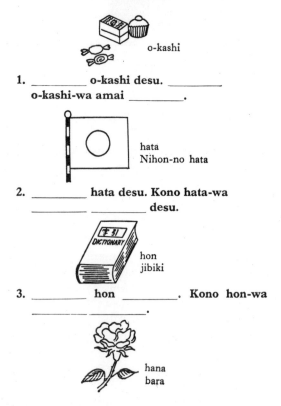

o-kashi

1. _____ o-kashi desu. _____

   o-kashi-wa amai _____.

   hata
   Nihon-no hata

2. _____ hata desu. Kono hata-wa

   _____ _____ desu.

   hon
   jibiki

3. _____ hon _____. Kono hon-wa

   _____ _____.

   hana
   bara

4. _____ hana _____.   _____
    hana-wa _____ desu.

o-kashi   cake, candy
hata   flag
Nihon-no hata   Japanese flag
jibiki   dictionary
bara   rose

LESSON 21

Adjectives

Keiyōshi   Adjectives

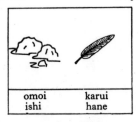

omoi   karui
ishi   hane

Kono ishi-wa omoi desu.   This stone is (these stones are) heavy.

Hane-wa karui desu.   A feather is (feathers are) light.

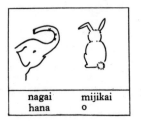

nagai   mijikai
hana   o

Zō-no hana-wa nagai desu. — An elephant's nose (trunk) is long.

Usagi-no o-wa mijikai desu. — A rabbit's tail is short.

hayai jetto   osoi densha

Jetto-wa hayai desu. — A jet plane is fast.

Densha-wa osoi desu. — A streetcar is slow.

hikui kodomo   takai otona

Kodomo-no sei-wa hikui desu. — A child's height is low. (A child is short.)

Otona-wa takai desu. — An adult is tall.

89

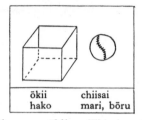

ōkii hako	chiisai mari, bōru

Kono hako-wa ōkii desu.   This box is large.

Kono mari-wa chiisai desu.   This ball is small.

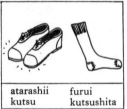

atarashii kutsu	furui kutsushita

Watakushi-no kutsu-wa atarashii desu.   My shoes are new.

Anata-no kutsushita-wa furui desu.   Your socks are old.

ishi	stone, rock
omoi	heavy
hane	feather
karui	light (in weight)

90

zō	elephant
nagai	long
usagi	rabbit
o	tail
mijikai	short
jetto	jet plane
hayai	fast
densha	streetcar
osoi	slow
kodomo	child, children
sei	height (of a person)
hikui	low, short (in height)
otona	adult, grown-up
takai	tall, high
hako	box
ōkii	large, big
mari, bōru	ball
chiisai	small, little
kutsu	shoes
atarashii	new
kutsushita	socks, stockings
furui	old

EXERCISE

1. Hane-wa omoi desuka. Iie, _____

_____ .

2. Zō-no hana-wa mijikai desuka. Iie,

_____ _____ .

3. Jetto-wa _____ desu. Densha-wa _____ desu.
4. Kono mari-wa ōkii desuka. Iie. _____ desu.
5. Anata-no kutsu-wa furui desuka. Iie, _____ _____.

LESSON 22

Adjectives and Adverbs

Keiyōshi	Fukushi	Adjective	Adverb
...i	...ku		
hayai	hayaku	fast, early	fast, early
osoi	osoku	slow, late	slowly, late
hikui	hikuku	low, short	low
takai	takaku	high, tall	high
omoi	omoku	heavy	heavily
karui	karuku	light	lightly
nagai	nagaku	long	long
mijikai	mijikaku	short	short
utsuku-shii	utsukushi-ku	beautiful	beautifully
ii (yoi)	yoku	good	well
akai	akaku	red	(no English equivalent)

NOTE: The formation and use of adverbs in Japanese is somewhat different from that in English. The chief difference to be noted here is that *narimasu* (become, becomes) and *narimashita* (became) are used with the adverb in Japanese rather than with the adjective as in English.

Watakushi-wa hayaku ikimasu.	I shall go quickly (early).
Watakushi-wa osoku kimashita.	I came late.
Ano hikōki-wa hiku-ku tobimasu.	That airplane is flying low.
Jetto-wa takaku tobi-mashita.	The jet plane flew high.
Nimotsu-ga omoku narimasu.	The luggage is getting (becoming) heavy.
Nimotsu-ga karuku narimashita.	The luggage became light.
Watakushi-wa nagaku Nihon-ni imasu.	I have been in Japan for a long time.
Watakushi-wa kami-no-ke-o mijikaku kirimashita.	I cut my hair short. (I had my hair cut short.)
Hana-wa utsukushiku sakimasu.	The flowers are bloom-ing beautifully.
Anata-wa Nihongo-ga yoku dekimasu.	You can speak Japanese well.
Ringo-wa akaku nari-masu.	The apples are turning (becoming) red.

kimashita	came
tobimasu	fly, flies
tobimashita	flew
narimasu	become, becomes

narimashita	became (got, turned, etc.)
imasu	am, is, are, have been, has been
kirimashita	cut (past tense)
sakimasu	bloom, blooms
ringo	apple, apples

EXERCISE

Adjectives:

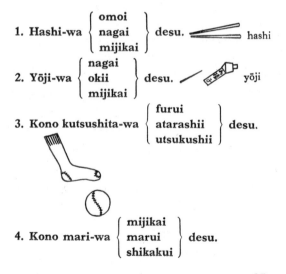

1. Hashi-wa $\left\{\begin{array}{l} \text{omoi} \\ \text{nagai} \\ \text{mijikai} \end{array}\right\}$ desu.   hashi

2. Yōji-wa $\left\{\begin{array}{l} \text{nagai} \\ \text{okii} \\ \text{mijikai} \end{array}\right\}$ desu.   yōji

3. Kono kutsushita-wa $\left\{\begin{array}{l} \text{furui} \\ \text{atarashii} \\ \text{utsukushii} \end{array}\right\}$ desu.

4. Kono mari-wa $\left\{\begin{array}{l} \text{mijikai} \\ \text{marui} \\ \text{shikakui} \end{array}\right\}$ desu.

5. **Kono hako-wa** $\left\{ \begin{array}{l} \textbf{nagai} \\ \textbf{shikakui} \\ \textbf{marui} \end{array} \right\}$ **desu.**

6. **Densha-wa** $\left\{ \begin{array}{l} \textbf{hayai} \\ \textbf{karui} \\ \textbf{osoi} \end{array} \right\}$ **desu.**

hashi	chopsticks
yōji	toothpick
marui	round
shikakui	square

Adjectives and Adverbs:

1. **Watakushi-ni kippu-o haya___ kudasai.**
2. **Yo___ gakusei-wa yo___ benkyō-o shi-masu.**
3. **Hikōki-wa taka___ tobimasu.**
4. **Fujisan-wa taka___ yama desu.**

96

5. Watakushi-wa atarashi___ yōfuku-o kai-mashita.
6. Watakushi-wa oso___ kimashita.
7. Watakushi-wa utsukushi___ keshiki-ga suki desu.
8. O-cha-ga tsumeta___ narimashita.
9. Atsu___ o-cha-o kudasai.
10. Kore-wa chiisa___ mari desu.

kippu	ticket
benkyō	study (noun)
benkyō-o shimasu	study, studies (verb)
shimasu	do, does
Fujisan	Mt. Fuji
keshiki	scenery

LESSON 23

Many and Much, Little and Few

takusan	many, much
sukoshi	a few, a little
sukoshi-mo (with negative verb)	none
Ringo-wa takusan arimasuka.	Are there a lot of apples? (Are there many apples?)

Hai, takusan arimasu.	Yes, there are a lot. (Yes, there are.)

Iie, takusan arimasen. Sukoshi arimasu.	No, there aren't many. There are a few.

Sukoshi-mo arima-sen.	There aren't any. (There are none.)

EXERCISE

1. **Gohan-wa takusan arimasuka. Hai,**
   _____ _____.

2. **Tori-wa takusan imasuka.** _____,
   _____ **imasu.**

3. **Anata-wa hon-o takusan motte-imasuka.**
   Hai, _____ **motte-imasu.**

99

4. **Isu-wa takusan arimasuka. Iie, _____
   arimasen. Ikutsu arimasuka. Hitotsu
   _____.**

5. **Ringo-wa mada takusan arimasuka. Iie,
   _____ arimasen.**

arimasu	is, are, there is, there are
arimasen	is not, are not, there is not, there are not
tori	bird
imasu	is, are (of living creatures)
ikutsu	how many?
hitotsu	one
mada	still, yet

LESSON 24

Where Is It?

Ichi	Position
tate	vertical
yoko	horizontal
-no ue-ni	on, on top of
-no naka-ni	in, inside

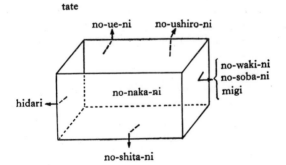

-no shita-ni	under, below
-no ushiro-ni	behind, in back of
-no soba-ni	by, beside, next to
-no waki-ni	by, beside, next to
migi	right
hidari	left

Doko-ni arimasuka.	Where is it?
Pen-wa doko-ni ari-masuka.	Where is the pen?

Pen-wa tsukue-no ue-ni arimasu.	The pen is on the desk.
Megane-wa doko-ni arimasuka.	Where are the eye-glasses?
Megane-wa hikida-shi-no naka-ni ari-masu.	The eyeglasses are in the drawer.
Denki-no suitchi-wa doko-ni arimasuka.	Where is the electric switch?

Sore-wa to-no waki-ni arimasu.	It is beside the door.
Hikōki-wa doko-o to-bimasuka.	Where does the airplane fly?

Hikoki-wa kumo-no ue-ni tobimasu.	The airplane flies above the clouds.
Ginkō-wa doko-ni ari-masuka.	Where is the bank?

Ginkō-wa kono michi-no hidari-gawa-ni arimasu.	The bank is on the left side of this street.
Yūbimbako-wa doko desuka.	Where is the mailbox?
Yūbimbako-wa migi-ni arimasu.	The mailbox is at (to) the right.

tsukue	desk
megane	eyeglasses
hikidashi	drawer
denki	electricity, electric light

denki-no	electric
suitchi	switch
doko-o	where (with objective postposition in this case—equivalent to English "sail the sea," "walk the streets," etc.)
kumo	cloud, clouds
ginkō	bank
michi	street, road
hidari-gawa	left side
migi-gawa	right side
yūbimbako	mailbox
migi-ni	at the right, to the right
hidari-ni	at the left, to the left

EXERCISE

1. **Mari-wa doko-ni arimasuka.** _____

_____ _____ _____.

2. **Megane-wa doko-ni arimasuka.** _____

_____ _____ _____.

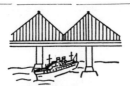

3. **Fune-wa doko desuka.** _____

_____ _____ _____.

4. **Panya-wa doko desuka.** _____

_____ _____ _____.

fune	boat, ship
hashi	bridge
panya	bakery shop

LESSON 25

Let's Call on the Telephone

Denwa-o kakemashō.   Let's call on the telephone.

John

JOHN: Moshi, moshi, Hanako-san desuka.   JOHN: Hello. Is this Hanako?

Hanako

HANAKO: Hai, sō desu.   HANAKO: Yes, it is.

JOHN: Watakushi-wa   JOHN: This is John.

John desu. Gokigen ikaga desuka.	How are you?
HANAKO: Watakushi-wa genki desu. Anata-wa ikaga desuka.	HANAKO: I'm fine. How are you?
JOHN: Watakushi-mo genki desu. Anata-wa Eigo-o hanasu-koto-ga dekimasu-ka?	JOHN: I'm fine too. Can you speak English?
HANAKO: Hai, sukoshi dekimasu. Anata-wa Nihongo-ga yoku dekimasu, ne.	HANAKO: Yes, I can— a little. You can speak Japanese well, can't you?
JOHN: Arigatō-gozaimasu. Dewa, sayonara.	JOHN: Thank you. Well then, goodbye.
HANAKO: Sayonara.	HANAKO: Goodbye.
denwa	telephone
denwa-o kakemasu	call (calls) on the telephone
kakemashō	let's call
moshi, moshi	hello (on the telephone)
Hanako	(common girl's name)
-san	Miss, Mr., Mrs. (never with one's own name)

watakushi-mo   I too

hanasu-koto   to speak, speaking (noun)

. . . ne   . . . don't you? . . . can't you? . . . isn't it? . . . aren't you? etc.

dewa   then, well then

LESSON 26

A Game and a Song

Jan-ken-pon is a very popular game among Japanese children as well as adults. The Japanese people play this game to decide the winner and the loser in everyday activities, just as the Americans flip a coin into the air to decide the same thing.

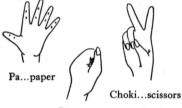

Pa...paper

Choki...scissors

Gū...stone

In this game, three hand signs are used: *gu*, symbolizing stone; *choki*, symbolizing scissors; and *pa*, symbolizing paper. The palm of the hand represents a sheet of paper and is called *pa*. The closed fist represents stone and is called *gu*. Two fingers—the index finger and the middle finger—represent a pair of scissors, called *choki*. Each player makes whichever of these gestures he chooses, and the winner

109

is decided as follows: Paper wraps stone, so paper wins over stone. Stone is too hard for scissors to cut, so stone wins over scissors. Scissors cut paper, so scissors win over paper.

Jan-ken-pon

As you play this game, you may sing the following well-known Japanese children's song:

Haru-ga Kita

1. Ha-ru-ga ki-ta, ha-ru-ga ki-ta. Doko-ni-ki-ta? Ya-ma-ni ki-ta, sa-to-ni ki-ta, no-ni-mo ki-ta.

2. To-ri-ga na-ku, to-ri-ga na-ku. Do-ko-de-na-ku? Ya-ma-de na-ku, sa-to-de na-ku, no-de-mo na-ku.

3. Ha-na-ga sa-ku, ha-na-ga sa-ku. Do-ko-ni sa-ku? Ya-ma-ni sa-ku, sa-to-ni sa-ku, no-ni-mo sa-ku.

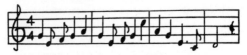

Ha ru ga ki ta, ha ru ga ki ta, Do ko ni ki ta?

Ya ma ni ki ta; Sa to ni ki ta; No ni mo ki ta.

110

haru	spring
-ga	(nominative postposition)
kita	has come, came
doko-ni	where
yama-ni	to (in) the mountains
sato-ni	to (in) the village
no-ni	to (in) the fields
-mo	too, also
tori	bird, birds
naku	sing, sings
doko-de	where
-de	(postposition indicating that an action is taking place at the location named)
hana	flowers
saku	bloom, blooms

Tango (Vocabulary)

All Japanese words used in this book are listed in this vocabulary except the numbers formed by combinations of other numbers, the numbers as used in counting people, the days of the month, and the months as counted (one month, two months, etc.).

ago	chin
aisatsu	greetings
aka-chan	baby
akai	red (adjective)
akaku	red (adverbial form)
aki	autumn
amai	sweet
ame	rain
Amerika-jin	an American, American people
anata	you
anata-ni	to you
anata-no	your
anata-wa	you (nominative)
ano	that (adjective, for distant objects)

are	that (pronoun, for distant objects)
are-wa	that (pronoun, nominative, for distant objects)
Arigatō.	Thank you. (less formal)
Arigatō-gozaimasu.	Thank you. (more formal)
arimasen	is not, are not, there is not, there are not
arimasu	is, are, there is, there are
asa	morning
ashi	leg, foot, legs, feet
ashi-no-yubi	toe, toes
ashita	tomorrow
asu	tomorrow
atama	head
atarashii	new
atatakai	warm
atsui	hot
ban	evening
bara	rose
bata	butter
benkyō	study (noun)
benkyō-shimashō	let's study (trans.)
benkyō-shimasu	study, studies (trans.)

LET'S STUDY JAPANESE

benkyō-o shimasu	study, studies (intrans.)
bijinesu-man	businessman
bōru	ball
bōshi	hat
bubun	part
byōki	sickness, ill
cha (usually **o-cha**)	tea
chiisai	small, little
de-arimasen	am not, is not, are not
deguchi	exit
dekimasen	be unable, cannot
dekimasu	be able, can
denki	electricity, electric light, electric
denki-no	electric
densha	streetcar
denwa	telephone
denwa-bangō	telephone number
denwa-o kakemasu	call on the telephone
deshita	was, were
desu	am, is, are
dewa	then, well then
dō	how?
dochira	which?
doko	where?
dōmo	very much

114

Do-yōbi	Saturday
dōzo	please
e	picture, painting
Eigo	English language
eki	station
empitsu	pencil
en	yen (360 yen=$1.00)
Fujisan	Mt. Fuji
fukushi	adverb
fun (pun)	minute
fune	boat, ship
furui	old
futatsu	two
fuyu	winter
-ga	(nominative postposition)
gaido	guide
gakkō	school
gakusei	student
genki	healthy, fine, well
geta	wooden clogs
ginkō	bank
go	five
Gochisō-sama.	(everyday expression said after eating)

Go-gatsu	May
gogo	afternoon, P.M.
gohan	cooked rice
gokigen	feeling, state of health
Gokigen ikaga desuka?	How are you?
Gomen-nasai.	I am sorry. Excuse me Pardon me.
gorufu	golf
gozen	morning, A.M.
gyūnyū	milk
ha	tooth, teeth
hachi	eight
Hachi-gatsu	August
hagaki	postcard
hai	yes
haizara	ashtray
hako	box
han	half
hana	flower
hana	nose
hanasu-koto	to speak, speaking (noun)
hane	feather
happi	happi coat
haru	spring
hashi	bridge
hashi (sometimes **o-hashi**)	chopsticks

hata	flag
hayai	fast, quick, early (adjective)
hayaku	fast, quickly, early (adverb)
hidari	left (direction)
hidari-gawa	left side
hikidashi	drawer
hikōki	airplane
hikui	low, short (in height)
hikuku	low (adverbial form)
hiru	afternoon, noon, P.M.
hitai	forehead
hitotsu	one
hiza	knee
hoho	cheek
hon	book
hoteru	hotel
hyaku	hundred
hyōgen	expression (in speech)
ichi	one
ichi	position
Ichi-gatsu	January
ii (sometimes **yoi**)	good, fine
iie	no (interjection)
ikaga	how?
ikimashō	let's go

ikimasu (sometimes go, goes
  yukimasu)

iku-koto (sometimes to go, going (noun)
  yuku-koto)

ikura how much?

ikutsu how many?

imasu is, are, am

imasen is not, are not, am not

inu dog

Irasshaimase. Welcome. Please come in.

iriguchi entrance

isha doctor

ishi stone, rock

isu chair

Itadakimasu. (everyday expression, said before eating)

itai painful

itsu when?

itsutsu five

jan-ken-pon (the Japanese game of "scissors, paper, and stone")

jetto jet plane

-ji o'clock, time

jibiki dictionary

jidōsha car

jū	ten
Jū-gatsu	October
Jū-ichi-gatsu	November
Jū-ni-gatsu	December
jūsho	address
-ka	(The sentence that ends with *-ka* is an interrogative sentence.)
kaban	suitcase, brief case
kabin	vase
kaimashita	bought
kaimono	shopping
kakimasu	write, writes
kaku-koto	to write, writing (noun)
kamera	camera
kami	paper
kami-no-ke	hair
kao	face
karada	body
karai	salty, peppery, spicy
karui	light (adjective)
karuku	lightly (adverb)
kasa	umbrella
kashi (sometimes **o-kashi**)	cake
kata	shoulder
katai	hard, crisp

kawaii	cute, lovely, pretty
Ka-yōbi	Tuesday
kazu	number
ke	hair
keiyōshi	adjective
keshiki	scenery
kikō	climate
kimashita	came
kimasu	come, comes
kinō	yesterday
kippu	ticket
kirai	dislike
kirimasu	cut (present tense)
kirimashita	cut (past tense)
kisetsu	season
kisha	train
kita	came, has come
kodomo	child, children
kōhii	coffee
koko, koko-ni	here
kokonotsu	nine
Komban-wa.	Good evening.
kongetsu	this month
Konnichi-wa.	Good day. Hello. Good afternoon.
kono	this (adjective)
konshū	this week
kore	this (pronoun)

kore-wa	this (pronoun, nominative)
kotae	answer
ku	nine
kubi	neck
kuchi	mouth
. . . kudasai	(please) give me
kumo	cloud
kumori	cloudy
kuru-koto	to come, coming (noun)
kutsu	shoes
kutsushita	stockings, socks
kyō	today
kyū	nine
kyūjitsu	holiday
mada	still, yet
mae	before, to (in telling time)
mari	ball
marui	round
me	eye, eyes
megane	eyeglasses
Meshi-agatte kudasai.	Please help yourself. Please do eat. (polite expression)
michi	street, road
migi	right (direction)

migi-gawa	right side
mijikai	short (adjective)
mijikaku	short (adverb)
mikan	tangerine
mimi	ear, ears
miruku	milk
mittsu	three
mizu (sometimes **o-mizu**)	water
-mo	too, also
Moku-yōbi	Thursday
moshi, moshi	hello (on the telephone)
motte-imasen	have not, has not
motte-imasu	have, has
mune	chest
mushi	insect
muttsu	six
nagai	long (adjective)
nagaku	long (adverb)
naka	inside (noun)
naku	cry, sing (birds)
namae	name
nan, nani	what?
nana, nanatsu	seven
narimashita	became, grew
narimasu	become, becomes, grow, grows

natsu	summer
. . . , ne	. . . , isn't it? . . . , aren't you? . . . , don't you? etc.
neko	cat
nezumi	mouse, rat
ni	two
-ni	to, at, in, for
nichi	day (date)
nichijō	daily, everyday
Nichi-yōbi	Sunday
Ni-gatsu	February
Nihon	Japan
Nihongo	Japanese language
Nihon-jin	a Japanese, Japanese people
Nihon-no hata	Japanese flag
Nihon ryōri	Japanese dishes (cooking)
niku	meat
nimotsu	luggage, package
ningyō	doll
no	field
-no	of, 's (possessive; postposition for possessive case)
nodo	throat
-no naka-ni	in, inside

-no shita-ni	under
-no soba-ni	by, beside, next to
-no ue-ni	on, to top of, over
-no ushiro-ni	behind
-no waki-ni	by, beside, next to
o	tail
o-	(honorific prefix often added to a noun for politeness)
o-cha	tea
Ohayō-gozaimasu.	Good morning.
o-hashi	chopsticks
oishii	tasty, delicious
o-kashi	cake, candy
ōkii	big, large
okusan	wife, Mrs.
o-mawari-san	policeman
Omedetō-gozaimasu.	Congratulations! (This expression is for any happy occasion such as a wedding, a birthday, New Year's Day, graduation, baby's arrival, etc.)
o-mizu	water
omoi	heavy
omoku	heavily

o-naka	stomach
ongaku	music
o-saji	spoon
o-satō	sugar
o-sembei	Japanese rice crackers
o-shio	salt
osoi	slow, late
osoku	slowly, late (adverb)
o-tenki	weather
o-tōfu	bean curd
otona	adult, grown-up
Oyasumi-nasai.	Good night.
pan	bread
panya	bakery shop
pen	pen
piano	piano
raigetsu	next month
raishū	next week
ringo	apple
roku	six
Roku-gatsu	June
ryōri	cooking
saji (sometimes **o-saji**)	spoon
sakana	fish
sakimasu	blooms, bloom

saku	blooms, bloom
samui	cold
san	three
-san	Mr., Mrs., Miss
San-gatsu	March
sato	village
satō (sometimes **o-satō**)	sugar
Sayonara.	Goodbye.
sei	height (of a person)
sembei (sometimes **o-sembei**)	Japanese rice crackers
sen	thousand
sengetsu	last month
sensei	teacher
senshū	last week
shashinki	camera
shi	four
shichi	seven
Shichi-gatsu	July
Shi-gatsu	April
shikakui	square
shimasu	do, does
shimbun	newspaper
shinju	pearl, pearls
shinsen	fresh
shio (sometimes **o-shio**)	salt
shiroi	white
shita	tongue

shita	bottom, lower part, foot (of hill)
-shō	let's, let us (verb ending)
shokki	dinnerware
shū	week
soba	side
soko, soko-ni	there
sono	that (adjective, for non-distant objects)
sore	that (pronoun, for non-distant objects)
sore-wa	that (pronoun, nominative, for non-distant objects)
sugi	after, past (in telling time)
suitchi	switch
suki de-arimasen	do not like, does not like
suki desu	like (verb)
sukoshi	a little, a few
sukoshi-mo	none
suzushii	cool
tabako	cigarette
tabemasu	eat, eats
tabemono	food
taberu-koto	to eat, eating (noun)

tadashii	right, correct
takai	high, tall
takaku	high (adverb)
takusan	many, much
tamago	egg
tango	vocabulary
tate	vertical
te	hand
tenki (sometimes **o-tenki**)	weather
to	door
to	and
tō	ten
tobimashita	flew
tobimasu	fly, flies (verb)
tōfu (sometimes **o-tōfu**)	bean curd
tokei	watch, clock
toki	time
Tōkyō	capital city of Japan
tomodachi (sometimes **o-tomodachi**)	friend
tori	bird
tōsuto	toast
tsuki	month
tsukue	desk
tsumetai	cool, cold
uchi	house, home

ude	arm
ue	top, upper part
usagi	rabbit
ushiro	back, rear (noun)
utsukushii	beautiful
utsukushiku	beautifully
uwagi	jacket, coat
-wa	(nominative postposition)
waki	side
warui	bad
watakushi-ni (watashi-ni)	to me
watakushi-no (watashi-no)	my
watakushi-wa (watashi-wa)	I
-ya	store, shop
yama	mountain
yasai	vegetable, vegetables
yattsu	eight
yawarakai	soft
yo, yon	four
yōbi	day of the week
yōfuku	clothes, dress (Western style)
yoi (usually **ii**)	good, fine

yōji	toothpick
yoko	horizontal
yoku	well
yomimasu	read, reads
yomu-koto	to read, reading (noun)
yoru	night
yottsu	four
yubi	finger
yūbimbako	mailbox
yūbin	mail
yūbinkyoku	post office
yūgata	evening
yuki	snow
yukimasu (usually **iki-masu**)	go, goes
yuku-koto (usually **iku-koto**)	to go, going (noun)
yūmei	famous
zō	elephant
zōri	sandals